Valley Forge: The History and Legacy of the Most Famous Military Camp of the Revolutionary War

By Charles River Editors

An illustration depicting Washington and Lafayette at Valley Forge

About Charles River Editors

Charles River Editors provides superior editing and original writing services across the digital publishing industry, with the expertise to create digital content for publishers across a vast range of subject matter. In addition to providing original digital content for third party publishers, we also republish civilization's greatest literary works, bringing them to new generations of readers via ebooks.

Sign up here to receive updates about free books as we publish them, and visit Our Kindle Author Page to browse today's free promotions and our most recently published Kindle titles.

Introduction

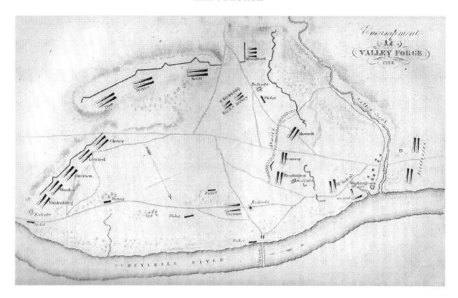

A contemporary map of the encampment

Valley Forge

"Naked and Starving as they are

We cannot enough admire

the Incomparable Patience and Fidelity

of the Soldiery." – George Washington

"And here, in this place of sacrifice, in this vale of humiliation, in this valley of the Shadow of Death out of which the Life of America rose, regenerate and free, let us believe with an abiding faith that to them Union will seem as dear, and Liberty as sweet, and Progress as glorious as they were to our fathers, and are to you and me, and that the institutions which have made us happy, preserved by the virtue of our children, shall bless the remotest generations of the time to come." – Henry Armitt Brown

Though Americans would be able to look back in hindsight at 1777 as the year the American Revolution reached a turning point in favor of the colonists, the winter of 1777 was still considered a miserable point for the cause at the time. Although Benedict Arnold and Horatio Gates were victorious at Saratoga, George Washington and his Continental army had been less successful. After being pushed back into Pennsylvania at the end of 1776, Washington attempted to surround the British army as it invaded Philadelphia in 1777, but he failed miserably. At the Battle of Germantown, Washington was defeated and forced to retreat, and on October 19th, 1777, the British entered Philadelphia and the Continental Congress fled to nearby York. Ultimately, it would be the French, not Washington, who forced the British out of Philadelphia. After learning of the French entry into the war, the British immediately abandoned Philadelphia to garrison New York City, which the British feared could be taken by French naval assault.

After another disappointing year of defeats, Washington's 11,000 men entered winter quarters at Valley Forge in Pennsylvania, about 20 miles outside of occupied Philadelphia. His army had repeatedly faced a lack of discipline and chronic disorganization, and Congress began to consider replacing Washington as Commander in Chief after the fall of Philadelphia. General Gates, who had received the lion's share of the credit for Saratoga by marginalizing Benedict Arnold's role in its success when he submitted his report to the Congress, was floated as an alternative, and Washington was understandably devastated. Making matters worse, the winter was unusually harsh, leading to an estimated 2,000 or so deaths in camp from diseases. Gouverneur Morris would later call the soldiers at Valley Forge a "skeleton of an army...in a naked, starving condition, out of health, out of spirits."

However, it was at Valley Forge that Washington truly forged his army. He introduced a more rigorous training program for his troops, sponsored by Prussian General Friedrich Wilhelm von Steuben, who had fought with Frederick the Great. Like the Marquis de Lafayette before him, von Steuben came to Washington's army via the recommendation of Benjamin Franklin, who hoped to use their appointments to curry political favor internationally. Despite speaking little English, von Steuben went about drafting a drill manual in French, and he personally presided over training drills and military parades. With the help of von Steuben, the Continental Army left Valley Forge in the spring of 1778 a more disciplined army than ever before, and the worst of Washington's failures were behind him.

Valley Forge: The History and Legacy of the Most Famous Military Camp of the Revolutionary War chronicles the history of the site and the camp that helped create America's first truly professional army. Along with pictures depicting important people, places, and events, you will learn about Valley Forge like never before.

Valley Forge: The History and Legacy of the Most Famous Military Camp of the Revolutionary War

About Charles River Editors

Introduction

Chapter 1: The Nation's Shrine

A map of Valley Forge, Philadelphia, and the movements of the 1777 Philadelphia Campaign

"The super-eminent distinction of Valley Forge lies in the fact that in the American Revolution it was the winter quarters of Washington and his patriot army in the trying winter of 1777-8. The encampment was for a period of exactly six months, from the 19th of December to the 19th of June. It is the story of this encampment, with its harrowing details of hardship and suffering, that has given to the locality its unique place in American history, and clothed it with patriotic interest wide-spread and enduring as the nation itself. Here no battle was fought, here no cruel ravages were wrought by onslaught of the enemy, but the trials endured and the human life here sacrificed on the altar of liberty during this, the most crucial period of the war for American Independence, render it eminently fitting, in history as in song, that the place should be extolled and venerated as: The Nation's Shrine." - James Riddle, *Valley Forge Guide and Handbook* (1910)

The Fall of 1777 was likely just as picturesque as any other in Pennsylvania. The leaves on the trees began to turn from a healthy green to the last beautiful colors that all too soon gave way to death. General George Washington was a farmer by nature and by trade and he was well accustomed to the rhythm of the seasons, so as each day brought a slightly cooler morning and slightly earlier nightfall, Washington knew he had a problem. His men had been marching and fighting for nearly the entire year, as far back as the surprise attack on Trenton on Christmas Day 1776, and they needed rest in a safe and quiet place to spend the winter. He had seen enough of war to know that he would likely lose more men to cold, disease, and privation than he had to bullets, and he needed to save every life that he could in order to fight again when the spring came.

In looking for a place to establish his winter camp, Washington came across a small community known as Valley Forge. Located 20 miles northwest of Philadelphia, it seemed like an ideal location; there was plenty of empty land around the village in which his men could build shelters, and it was close enough to the British lines to keep an eye on their movements while being far enough away to keep them from attacking in force.

At the time, not everyone was pleased with Washington's choice of location for his winter quarters. Joseph Reed, the Adjutant-General of the Continental Army, wrote to the President of the Pennsylvania legislature, "A line of winter-quarters has been proposed and supported by some of his [Washington's] principal officers; but I believe I may assure you he will not come into it, but take post as near the enemy, and cover as much of the country as the nakedness and wretched condition of some part of the army will admit. To keep the field entirely is impracticable, and so you would think if you saw the plight we were in. You will soon know the plan, and as it has been adopted principally upon the opinions of the gentlemen of this State, I hope it will give satisfaction to you and the gentlemen around you. If it is not doing what we would, it is doing what we can; and I must say the general has shown a truly feeling and patriotic respect for us on this occasion, in which you would agree with me, if you knew all the circumstances."

While Reed pointed out the weakness of the army, another author noted the exposed condition of the camp at Valley Forge: "Washington's camp was by no means difficult of access; far less so than the posts occupied by him at the Brandywine; and in one part of the front the ascent was scarcely perceptible, and his rear was commanded by higher ground. His ditches were not three feet in depth ; nor was there a drummer in the British army, who could not, with the utmost ease, leap over them, and his defenses might have been battered down with fix- pounders. This is not an exaggerated picture of the rebel army, nor of the weakness of its situation. ... Upon these facts I leave the candour of the public to find, if it can be found, a reason why the [British] General did not attack, or surround, and take by siege, Washington's whole army. His numbers were greater than those of the rebels, who surrounded and took a British army, under General Burgoyne, of 400; veteran troops, in a situation not so distressful as that of Washington."

On November 25, 1777, the Continental Congress passed two resolutions that, while it did not seem so at the time, would soon become intricately related. The first proclaimed "that Genl Washington be directed to publish in Genl Orders, that Congress will speedily take into Consideration the Merits of such Officers who have distinguished themselves by their Intrepidity and attention to the health and Discipline of their Men, and adopt such Regulations as shall tend to introduce Order and good Discipline into the Army, and to render the Situation of the Officers and Soldiers with respect to their cloathing and other Necessaries more eligible than it has hitherto been."

The second resolution was more prosaic: "For as much as it is the indispensable duty of all Men to adore the Superintending Providence of Almighty God to acknowledge with Gratitude their Obligations to him for Benefits received and to implore such further Blessings as they stand in need of and it having pleased him in his abundant Goodness and Mercy not only to continue to us the innumerable Bounties of his common Providence, but also to smile upon us in the Prosecution of a Just and necessary War for the Defence of our Invaluable Rights and Liberties, It is therefore recommended by Congress that Thursday the 18 December next be set apart for solemn thanksgiving and praise that at one Time and with one Voice, the good People may express the grateful Feelings of their Hearts and consecrate themselves to the Service of their divine Benefactor, and that together with their sincere Acknowledgments and Offerings they may Join a penitent Confession of their Sins, and Supplications for such further Blessings they stand in need of. The Chaplains will properly notice this Recommendation that the Day of Thanksgiving may be duly observed in the Army agreeable to the Intentions of Congress."

Of course, when Washington arrived in Valley Forge on the day after this day of "solemn thanksgiving and praise," he knew only too well that his men would need more than prayers if they were to win the new country's independence.

If anything, Washington made his winter camp just in time, because his army was in desperate need. To illustrate this point, the following story was later told: "The officer commanding the detachment, choosing the most favorable ground, paraded his men to pay their General the honors of a passing salute. As Washington rode slowly up, he was observed to be eying very earnestly something that attracted his attention on the frozen surface of the road. Having returned the salute with that native grace and dignified manner that won the admiration of the soldiers of the Revolution, the Chief reined in his charger, and ordering the commanding officer of the detachment to his side, addressed him as follows: 'How comes it, sir, that I have tracked the march of your troops by the blood-stains of their feet upon the frozen ground? Were there no shoes in the commissary's stores that this sad spectacle is to be seen along the public highway?' The officer replied: 'Your Excellency may rest assured that this sight is as painful to my feelings as it can be to yours, but there is no remedy within our reach. When shoes were issued the different regiments were served in turn; it was our misfortune to be among the last to be served, and the stores became exhausted before we could obtain even the smallest supply.' The General was observed to be deeply affected by his officer's description of the soldiers' privations and sufferings. His compressed lips, the heaving of his manly chest betokened the powerful emotions that were struggling in his bosom, when, turning towards the troops, with a voice tremulous, yet kindly, he exclaimed, 'poor fellows!' Then giving rein to his horse he rode rapidly away."

A picture of the perimeter of the camp looking southeast towards Philadelphia

A picture of a cannon and redan pointed southeast towards the British lines at Philadelphia

Chapter 2: Rapid Construction

"The troops under the immediate command of General Washington were those comprised in what was designated as the Middle department of the Continental Army — the Northern and Southern departments being commanded separately by generals appointed to the position by Congress, but subject to the Commander-in-Chief. In all respects Washington's was the department preeminent. ... The winter of 1777-8 was one of unusual severity, and by the 19th of December, which marked the arrival of the troops at Valley Forge, the severe weather had already set in. With only tents in the meantime to shelter them from wintry wind and snow, and with but scant supply of blankets and clothing, the men nevertheless drove them-selves heroically to the work of establishing their quarters. The first undertaking was not, as one might imagine, the fortification of the camp against approach from the enemy, but the more humane one — the erection of log cabins or huts to take the place as speedily as possible of the cheerless tents for the men; the throwing up of entrenchments and the construction of earth forts and redoubts for the defense of the encampment came later. Prizes were offered to the soldiers by the Commander-in-Chief for rapid construction, and best method of roofing, and everything was done to stimulate activity in the work." - James Riddle, *Valley Forge Guide and Handbook* (1910)

When Washington and his men finally arrived at Valley Forge, they found little to welcome them. While a few of the townspeople surrendered their homes or at least a room or two for the officers' use, the vast majority of the men had to build their own shelter. This may not have been as bad as it sounds given that most of them had built homes in the wilderness before, but the terrible weather made their task both urgent and daunting. Washington quickly issued orders: "The Major Genl, accompanied by the Engenieurs (engineers) are to view the Ground attentively and fix upon the proper spott for hutting so as to render the Camp as strong & inaccessible as possible, the Engenieurs after this are to mark the ground out and direct the Field Officers appointed to Superintend the Building for each Brigade where they are to be placed. The Soldiers in cutting their fire wood are to Save such parts of each Tree as will do for building, Reserving sixteen and 18 feet of the Trunk for Logs to Rear their Huts with. In doing this each Reg[iment] is to reap the benefit of its own Labour — All those who in consequence of the orders of the 18 [ft] Instant have turned their thoughts to an easy and expeditious manner of Covering their Huts are requested to Communicate their plans to Maj' Gen! Sullivan, Greene or Lord Sterling who will cause experiments to be made and assign the proffer'd reward to the best projector." In addition to wood, the soldiers also gathered straw: "The Q.M.G. (Quartermaster General) is to delay no time but use his utmost exertion to procure large Quantities of Straw Either for Covering the Huts if it should be found necessary or for beds for the soldiers. He is to assure the farmers that unless they get their Grain thresh'd out Imediately the Straw will be taken with the Grain in it and paid for as Straw only."

Washington was respectful of the needs of the farmers living around him, but he knew the army was fighting for their freedom and thus had no qualms demanding that they do their part. On December 20, he ordered, "By virtue of the power and direction especially given, I hereby enjoin and require all persons residing within seventy miles of my headquarters to thresh one-half of their grain by the first day of March next ensuing, on pain, in case of failure, of having all that shall remain in sheaves, after the period above mentioned, seized by the Commissaries and Quartermasters of the army, and paid for as straw."

Knowing it was critical to have all outdoor activities completed as soon as possible, Washington likewise ordered, "The Q.M. Genl is to collect as soon as possible all the Tents not now used by the Troops as soon as they are Hutted all the residue of the Tents & have them wash'd and dried & laid up in store such as are good for the next Campaign the others for the use which shall be directed the whole and be carefully preserved. The Col. and Officers Commanding Regiments are immediately to make return to the Q M Genl of every Tent belonging to their Reg., the Army being come to a fix'd Station. The Brigadiers and Officers Commanding Brigades are immediately to take effectual measures to collect and bring to Camp all the Officers and Soldiers scattered about the Country all the Officers are enjoined to see that their men do not wantonly or Needlessly burn and destroy rails and never to fire their sheds or huts when they leave them."

In his guide to Valley Forge, James Riddle described the finished products: "The huts, 14 x 16 feet in dimensions, were made to accommodate 12 private soldiers, and were arranged in rows, or streets. The officers were housed in similar quarters, but with less crowding, according to their rank, the generals each having a hut to himself. Each hut had a fireplace with log and clay chimney at the end opposite the entrance, and the bunks were arranged on the sides in tiers. Two small windows, with oiled paper for glass, admitted the light. The chinks between the logs were filled with clay, or mortar. Straw, supported by stakes or poles, was the material principally used for roofing, but it was hard to obtain, and for a time the use of the tents for roof-covering was resorted to. Straw also was needed as bedding- for the bunks.... The erection of seven or eight hundred such huts, with many larger buildings for Commissary, Artificer, and hospital purposes, together with suitable stabling for the horses, was the task to which the half-clad, half-provisioned men were obliged to apply themselves — a task which lingered on their hands through half the dreary winter."

Replicas of the cabins constructed for common soldiers

Pictures of the replicated inside of common soldiers' cabins at Valley Forge

Pictures of the replicated inside of an officer's cabin at Valley Forge

Replica of ovens used at Valley Forge

While his men were building huts and establishing their homes for the next six months, Washington was busy establishing order in the camp. To that end, on December 22, 1777, he published the General Orders for the camp. His first concern was to hang on to his soldiers, many of whom were growing discouraged and considering desertion. Moreover, some reasoned that if they were going to stay in the same place for the winter, they might as well return home and live with their families until it was time to fight again. To keep the men in camp, he ordered, "The good of the service requiring at this time, the attention of officers and soldiers to duty, the General orders, that no furloughs be granted to officers above the rank of Captain, but from himself; nor to those below that rank, but from the Major General, or Officer commanding the division, they belong to: Noncommissioned Officers and privates may be furloughed by their respective Brigadiers, or officers commanding brigades. But the General does in most express and positive terms, enjoin the Major Generals and Brigadiers, to grant furloughs only in case of absolute necessity, and even then to have proper regard to the state and condition of the regiment and company, before they are given. All furloughs to officers are to be registered by the Adjutant of the regiment; and those to non-commissioned officers and soldiers, by the commanding officer of the company they belong to, or they will not be deemed valid. The strictest punctuality, in returning, at the expiration of their furloughs will be required of all those who obtain them."

Washington also made provisions for allowing his men to move about the countryside freely so that they could continue to monitor the movements of the British: "Major General Sullivan having obligingly undertaken the direction of a bridge to be built over the Schuylkill, is to be excused from the common duties of the camp."

However, there was another concern, one that involved both morale and practicality. Washington did not have enough arms for his men, a situation he did not wish to draw attention to, but at the same time, soldiers obviously expected to have weapons. Washington found a creative solution to this problem by ordering, "As the proper arming of the officers would add considerable strength to the army, and the officers themselves derive great confidence from being armed in time of action, the General orders every one of them to provide himself with a half-pike or spear, as soon as possible; firearms when made use of withdrawing their attention too much from the men; and to be without either, has a very awkward and unofficerlike appearance. That these half-pikes may be of one length and uniformly made, the Brigadiers are to meet at General Maxwell's quarters tomorrow at 10 o'clock in the forenoon and direct their size and form. ... Any soldier who shall be found discharging his musket without leave, and in an irregular manner, is to receive 20 lashes immediately on the spot."

The men had barely finished their most rudimentary buildings when word came that they might have to go out again to meet the British. It may be surprising that many men were happy to hear the news, but General Jedediah Huntington explained, "Fighting will be far preferable to starving. My brigade are out of provisions, nor can the commissary obtain any meat. I have used every argument my imagination can invent to make the soldiers easy, but I despair of being able to do it much longer." Continental Army General James Varnum echoed that sentiment: "It's a very pleasing circumstance to the division under my command, that there is a probability of their marching; three days successively we have been destitute of bread. Two days we have been entirely without meat. The men must be supplied, or they cannot be commanded." However, as it turned out, the march proved unnecessary and the men were left to continue their building projects.

A picture of Varnum's headquarters at Valley Forge

Chapter 3: Unfit For Duty

"A smoke nuisance, resulting from the burning of wood in the many fires of the camp, was the cause of serious annoyance much of the time, affecting unfavorably not only the eyes and throats of the soldiers, but their patience and temper as well. The prevalence, moreover, of bad sanitary conditions, unavoidable except by the most rigid enforcement of camp regulations, was a menace still more serious. Sickness and disease, including fever and small-pox, soon invaded the camp, and death, with the solemn military burial ceremony, became an every-day occurrence. Fully 3000, it is estimated, died during the six months of the encampment. At the beginning of this period fourteen brigades of troops, representing a maximum of 17,000 men, were encamped within the lines. The precise number was 11,089, of which at that time 2898, according to Washington's report to Congress, December 23d, 'were unfit For duty, because they were barefoot and otherwise naked.' As weeks wore on the number of men fit for service was still further reduced by exposure, lack of provisions, desertion, sickness and death to the pitiable figure of 5012." - James Riddle, *Valley Forge Guide and Handbook* (1910)

One of the problems that has plagued military leaders from the dawn of time to the present is the natural conflict that often arises when armies of tired, hungry, and often lonely men are stationed near civilian populations. Around the time the encampment was built, word came that several farms had been robbed by hungry soldiers, and while Washington had no compunction about taking from local farms supplies that he felt he had to have to keep his men alive, he was committed to keeping order, paying for the items, and treating those with whom he dealt with respect. On December 26, he wrote, "It is with inexpressible grief and indignation that the General has received information of the cruel outrages and robberies lately committed by soldiers, on the other side of the Schuylkill: Were we in an enemy's country such practices would be unwarrantable; but committed against our friends are in the highest degree base, cruel, and injurious to the cause in which we are engaged. They demand therefore, and shall receive the severest punishment. Such crimes have brought reproach upon the army; and every officer and soldier suffers by the practices of such villains; and 'tis the interest, as well as duty, of every honest man to detect them, and prevent a repetition of such crimes. The General earnestly desires the General Officers, and those commanding Corps, to represent to their men, the cruelty, baseness and wickedness, of such practices, and the injury they do the army, and the common cause."

Determined to see to it that all future problems be kept to a minimum, Washington gave the following orders:

> "1st. That no officer, under the degree of a Field Officer, or officer commanding a regiment, give passes to non-commissioned officers or soldiers, on any pretense whatever.

> 2nd. That no non-commissioned officer, or soldier, have with him, arms of any kind, unless he is on duty.

> 3rd. That every non-commissioned officer, or soldier, caught without the limits of the camp, not having such pass, or with his arms, shall be confined and severely punished.

> 4th. That the rolls of each company be called frequently, and that every evening, at different times, between the hours of eight and ten o'clock, all the men's quarters be visited, by such officers as the Brigadiers or the Officers commanding corps, shall daily appoint, and all absentees are to be exemplarily punished.

> 5th. That as some of the villains complained of, have been found mounted upon wagon horses; every wagon-master and conductor of wagons, is constantly to be near his charge, and frequently, particularly every evening and morning, to

inspect his wagons, and horses, and see that neither they, nor the wagoners are missing; and if a wagoner, or any of his horses are missing, and not on duty, he is to be confined and punished."

While he was strict when the need arose, Washington was also well aware that he was leading a group of farmers and tradesmen, not professional soldiers, and ultimately he had little to hold them with beyond their commitment to the cause of freedom. Therefore, having for the most part confined many to camp, a few days later he rewarded them: "[A] gill of spirits to be served this afternoon to each non-commissioned officer and soldier. And as officers may find it difficult and expensive to procure spirits for their own use in camp, he authorizes those of each regiment, to depute and send one of their own corps into this, or the neighbouring State, to purchase such spirits, and other articles for their accommodation in camp, as they shall find convenient for their own use only."

The liquor may have provided some comfort, but there was little other, and the men were almost always hungry. Mostly frontiersmen, they were accustomed to hunting for meat during the spring and summer and living off livestock during the colder months, but there was little livestock to butcher in the camp, and the men were dependent on terrible items such as "firecake." This was nothing more than flour mixed with water and baked over an open fire. Better days would see pepper pot soup served, but that was little more than a broth made from tripe and flavored with black pepper. It is not surprising, therefore, that Washington wrote to the Continental Congress on December 23, 1777, "Sir: Full as I was in my representation of matters in the Commissary department yesterday, fresh, and more powerful reasons oblige me to add, that I am now convinced, beyond a doubt that unless some great and capital change suddenly takes place in that line, this Army must inevitably be reduced to one or other of these three things. Starve, dissolve, or disperse, in order to obtain subsistence in the best manner they can; rest assured Sir this is not an exaggerated picture, but [and] that I have abundant reason to support what I say. Yesterday afternoon…I order'd the Troops to be in readiness…when, behold! to my great mortification, I was not only informed, but convinced, that the Men were unable to stir on Acct. of Provision, and that a dangerous Mutiny begun the Night before, and with difficulty was suppressed by the spirited exertion's of some officers was still much to be apprehended on acct. of their want of this Article. This brought forth the only Corny. in the purchasing Line, in this Camp; and, with him, this Melancholy and alarming truth; that he had not a single hoof of any kind to Slaughter, and not more than 25. Barls. of Flour! From hence form an opinion of our Situation when I add, that, he could not tell when to expect any."

Not only were there no animals with which to feed the soldiers, there was precious little available to feed the animals, and soon the horses were becoming weak. As December gave way to 1778, the army was becoming increasingly desperate for basic supplies. Even water was in short supply, to the extent the men had to depend on melting snow for drinking. This was a problem, because even though the winter was cold and frosty, there was not a lot of snow. Thus,

Washington kept pressing the Continental Congress, trying again to convince the powers that be that the men could not survive, much less fight, unless they were fed: "All I could do under these circumstances was, to send out a few light Parties to watch and harrass the Enemy, whilst other Parties were instantly detached different ways to collect, if possible, as much Provision as would satisfy the present pressing wants of the Soldiery. But will this answer? No Sir: three or four days bad weather would prove our destruction. What then is to become of the Army this Winter? and if we are as often without Provisions now, as with it, what is to become of us in the Spring, when our force will be collected, with the aid perhaps of Militia, to take advantage of an early Campaign before the Enemy can be reinforced?"

Hoping that he had made a point, Washington used uncharacteristically strong language, going so far as to admit that he was tired of being blamed for the incompetence of others: "These are considerations of great magnitude, meriting the closest attention, and will, when my own reputation is so intimately connected, and to be affected by the event, justify my saying that [either] the present Commissaries are by no means equal to the execution [of their Office] or that the disaffection of the People is past all belief. The misfortune however does in my opinion, proceed from both causes, and though I have been tender heretofore of giving any opinion, or lodging complaints, as the change in that department took place contrary to my judgment, and the consequences thereof were predicted; yet, finding that the inactivity of the Army, whether for want of provisions, Clothes, or other essentials, is charged to my Account, not only by the common vulgar, but those in power, it is time to speak plain in exculpation of myself; with truth then I can declare that, no Man, in my opinion, ever had his measures more impeded than I have, by every department of the Army."

Washington used strong words for a good reason; he knew only too well that men weakened by malnutrition could not fight off the enemy and were also easy prey for illness. At the same time, he also knew that he served at the pleasure of the Continental Congress, so he rushed to present evidence that his were not just the rambling complaints of an overburdened general in over his head.

That said, seeing his men sleeping night after night on damp, festering ground was enough to anger him, and he enumerated each of the offences against his efforts: "Since the Month of July, we have had no assistance from the Quarter Master Genl. and to want of assistance from this department, the Commissary Genl. charges great part of his deficiency; to this I am to add, that notwithstanding it is a standing order (and often repeated) that the Troops shall always have two days Provisions by them, that they may be ready at any sudden call, yet, no opportunity has scarce[ly] ever yet happened of taking advantage of the Enemy that has not been either totally obstructed or greatly impeded on this Acct., and this…great and crying evil is not all."

Washington then went on to name the many items, other than food, that his men depended on: "Soap, Vinegar and other Articles allowed by Congress we see none of nor have [we] seen

[them] I believe since the battle of Brandywine; the first indeed we have now little occasion of [for] few men having more than one Shirt, many only the [half] of one, and Some none at all…"

While the food was an obvious necessity, Washington and his men were facing a long, hard winter during which common soldiers would be sheltered in substandard accommodations. Warm clothes were an obvious necessity, but the army did not have them. At one point, as many as 4,000 men had to report as unfit for duty simply because they did not having enough clothing to cover themselves or shoes to wear. Washington complained, "[I]n addition to which as a proof of the little benefit received from a Clothier Genl., and at the same time as a further proof of the inability of an Army under the circumstances of this, to perform the common duties of Soldiers (besides a number of Men confined to Hospitals for want of Shoes, and others in farmers Houses on the same Acct.) we have, by a field return this day made no less than 2898 Men now in Camp unfit for duty because they are bare foot and otherwise naked and by the same return it appears that our whole strength in continental Troops (Including the Eastern Brigades which have joined us since the surrender of Genl. Burgoyne) exclusive of the Maryland Troops sent to Wilmington amount to no more than 8200 In Camp fit for duty. Notwithstanding which, and that, since the 4th Instant, our Numbers fit for duty from the hardships and exposures they have undergone, particularly on Acct. of Blankets (numbers being obliged and [still are to] set up all Night by fires, instead of taking comfortable rest in a natural way) have decreased near 2000 Men."

Washington concluded with a daring charge: "[W]e find Gentlemen…reprobating the measure as much as if they thought Men were made of Stocks or Stones and equally insensible of frost and Snow and moreover, as if they conceived it practicable for an inferior Army under the disadvantages I have described ours to be which is by no means exaggerated to confine a superior one (in all respects well appointed, and provided for a Winters Campaign) within the City of Philadelphia, and cover from depredation and waste the States of Pennsylvania, [New] Jersey, etc. But what makes this matter still more extraordinary in my eye is, that these very Gentlemen who were well apprised of the nakedness of the Troops, from occular demonstration [who] thought their own Soldiers worse clad than others, and advised me, near a Month ago, to postpone the execution of a Plan I was about to adopt (in consequence of a resolve of Congress) for seizing Clothes, under strong assurances that an ample supply would be collected in ten days agreeably to a decree of the State not one Article of which, by the bye, is yet come to hand, should think a Winters Campaign and the covering these States from the Invasion of an Enemy so easy a business. I can assure those Gentlemen that it is a much easier and less distressing thing to draw remonstrances in a comfortable room by a good fire side than to occupy a cold bleak hill and sleep under frost and Snow without Clothes or Blankets; however, although they seem to have little feeling for the naked, and distressed Soldier, I feel superabundantly for them, and from my Soul pity those miseries, which it is neither in my power to relieve or prevent."

Fortunately, the Congress heard his words, though it moved in the slow, methodical way that large political organizations always seem to when carrying on their business. On January 24,

1778, five representatives from Congress arrived in Valley Forge to assess the situation for themselves and report back their findings, and they were so thoroughly shocked by what they saw that they agreed to Washington's request that the Congress itself take over the purchase and distribution of supplies.

Within a month, the situation in camp had improved, at least as far as food and clothes went, but by then, many of the illnesses that resulted due to exposure and overcrowding had taken their toll. Concerned about his men personally, and as a fighting force, Washington instructed one of his officers on April 4, 1778, "You are to visit all the Hospitals of which I have given you a list, and such others in the States of Pennsylvania and [New] Jersey as may have been omitted, if there are Continental Soldiers in them. You are to bring me an exact account of the state of each hospital with the number of Men therein; distinguishing the State, Regiment, and Company they belong to; and, as nearly as possible, those who died in, and have been discharged from them. For this purpose you are authorized to examine, if necessary, the Books of the Directors, Surgeons, Commissaries, etc. You are to make a minute enquiry into the management of the Sick; the care and attendance given them; their wants; etc. and report the same to me with your opinion of the number and proper place or places to fix the Hospitals at for the purposes of accommodating the Sick, the more convenient superintending of them; and reducing the expense by lessening the number of Physicians, Surgeons, etc., etc., which are now employed and may be necessary in the present divided state of the Hospitals. You are to inform yourself truly of the number of Soldiers employed as Guards, Tenders of the Sick, Waiters on Officers, Surgeons, etc., and, if it shall appear to you that any are improperly employed order them to their respective Regiments and in such a manner as to be known whether the order is complied with or not. The Arms and accoutrements at each Hospital is also to become an object of your attention."

By this time, Washington had lost more men to typhoid, typhus, dysentery and pneumonia than he had to bayonets and bullets. One anonymous author, writing in 1780, admitted, "The camp-disorder (dysentery) raged among his men, which obliged [Washington] to establish no less than eleven hospitals; and many died, many deserted to their several provinces, and near 3000 or them came over to the British army. From these circumstances, his army was reduced, before the month of March, to less than 4000 men, and by far the greater part of these were in a manner naked, many without shoes or stockings, and but few, except the Virginians, with the necessary clothing. His horses were in a condition yet worse; they were constantly exposed to showers of rain, and falls of show, both day and night, many of them died; the rest were so emaciated as to be unfit for labour, and, in addition to this distressful situation, Washington had not in his camp, at any one time, one week's provisions either for man or horse, and sometimes his men were totally destitute."

Hoping to stave off disease as much as possible, Washington ordered as many of his men as possible be vaccinated for smallpox, and this certainly saved some lives. However, then as now, there were some who refused to be vaccinated, which heightened the outbreak of the disease in camp. As such, Washington was determined to find out who was healthy and get them back into action, especially as the time for attack approached: "Herewith you will receive a Copy of the Instructions given to the Officers sent to the different Hospitals. Enquire how far they have been complied with, and, if you should discover any inattention or neglect in any of them, order them immediately to Camp with proofs of their Misconduct if you should think a Court Martial proper. Above all things, you are to cause every Officer and Soldier at any of the Hospitals who are fit for duty, and not detained at them by order, or to answer any valuable purpose to repair to Camp immediately, and join their respective Corps; this you will likewise do by all such as you may meet with in your circuit under the like circumstances. Your expenses, in the course of this tour of duty, will be borne by the public; an Acct. of which you will render to the Auditors; economy, and every dispatch which you can use consistent with the valuable purposes of your journey will be expected, as the Season is fast advancing and every Officer will be found necessary at his post in the line. Note, If at any of the Hospitals you shall visit, there should be found Soldiers unfit for Service, and whose appearance affords little hope of their ever becoming useful to the States in that line you are at liberty to discharge them provided it is agreeable to their own desires."

Chapter 4: Months of Toil, Hardship, and Suffering

"To form some conception of the burden which rested upon the mind and heart of the Commander-in-Chief during the progress of these months of toil, hardship, and suffering, requires but little brilliancy of imagination. Always profoundly sympathetic in his attitude toward his men, his sympathy during these dark days was rendered the keener, and its reciprocal effect the weightier, from a sense of his inability to furnish needed relief. When we have added to this the strain of his multitudinous and diversified official labors, what he endured from the criminal apathy and inaction of Congress, the blundering stupidity of the Commissary Department, the malignity of private and public criticism, the outcropping of bitter envy and jealousy in some of his subordinate officers, the secret hatching of high-handed conspiracy to deprive him of the Army's command, and other causes of aggravation quite as noteworthy, there is given us some conception of the by no means enviable task which during these six months constituted the lot of Gen. Washington. It is here also, as we witness his patient, placid and resolute spirit in the midst of it all, that we catch a glimpse of the colossal stature of the man, soldier and statesman, in whom were centered the hopes and fortune of the United States in the struggle for independence." - James Riddle, *Valley Forge Guide and Handbook* (1910)

Despite improvements in the army's provisions, the situation at Valley Forge remained desperate. Years later, then Chief Justice of the United States Supreme Court John Marshall observed that at no other time "had the American Army been reduced to a situation of greater peril than during the winter at Valley Forge. More than once they were absolutely without food. Even while their condition was less desperate in this respect, their stock of provisions was so scanty that there was seldom at any time in the stores a quantity sufficient for the use of the troops for a week. Consequently had the enemy moved out in force the American Army could not have continued in camp. The want of provisions would have forced them out of it; and their deplorable condition with respect to clothes, disabled them from keeping the field in winter. The returns of the first of February exhibit the astonishing number of 3,989 men in camp unfit for duty for want of clothes. Of this number scarcely a man had a pair of shoes. Even among those returned capable of duty, very many were so badly clad that exposure to the colds of the season must have destroyed them. Although the total of the army exceeded 17,000 men, the present effective rank and file amounted to only 5,012. The returns throughout the winter did not essentially vary from that which has been particularly stated."

By this time, many among the American people had begun to criticize Washington and even call for his replacement. Some felt that General Horatio Gates, the hero of the Battle of Saratoga, would do a better job, including Gates himself, who frequently angled for the job by criticizing Washington. Brigadier General Thomas Conway had also been working for some time to undermine Washington, and he was joined in his efforts by Dr. Benjamin Rush, one of the signers of the Declaration of Independence. On January 12, 1778, Rush complained about Washington in a letter to the prominent Virginian politician Patrick Henry, "The northern army has shown us what Americans are capable of doing with a GENERAL at their head. The spirit of the southern army is no ways inferior to the spirit of the northern. A Gates, a Lee, or a Conway would in a few weeks render them an irresistible body of men. A Gates, a Lee or a Conway would, in a few weeks render them an irresistible body of men. The of the above officers had accepted of the new office of inspector general of our army, in order to reform abuses; but the remedy I only a palliative one. In one of his letters to a friend, he says, 'a great and good God hath decreed America to be free, or the [general] and weak counsellors would have ruined her long ago.'"

Gates

Conway

Henry

For his own part, Washington wrote of Conway, "General Conway's merit, then, as an Officer, and his importance in this Army, exist more in his own imagination than in reality: For it is a maxim with him, to leave no service of his own untold, nor to want anything which is to be obtained by importunity.... To Sum up the whole, I have been a Slave to the service: I have undergone more than most Men are aware of, to harmonize so many discordant parts, but it will be impossible for me to be of any further service, if such insuperable difficulties are thrown in my way...."

Conway and his cronies were obviously jealous of Washington, as made clear in "Thoughts of a Freeman", a paper sent to Congress that winter. In it, the author attacked Washington's leadership and went so far as to blame the general for the poor health of his men: "That the proper methods of attacking, beating and conquering the Enemy has never as yet been adapted by the Commander in C—f. That More men will dye this winter then it would have cost lives to have conquered the Enemy last Summer and fall. That it is better to dye honourably in the field then in a stinking Hospital. That the many Fruitless and unaccountable marches has had a great tendency to fill the Hospitals with Sick. That the Baggage has many times been sent away to the great hurt of the health of the Army. That contrary to the good old maxim, Raiment has been regarded more than life. That the general contempt shown to the Militia by the standing forces is a dangerous Omen. ... That the Carriages, horses and Harness belonging to the Army are in a very bad condition. That the greatest part of the Horses will be unfit for service before spring, if better methods of procuring Forage are not speedily adapted. That the present place of Encampment is illy chosen on account of Forage, etc. That there is too much Forage left within reach of the Enemy, though even yet a great deal of it might be brought off."

Having said all this, the author moved on to his demand that Washington be removed and, one can assume, replaced with either the author himself or one of his friends: "That if there is no General fit and willing to lead on the said attack, the said power ought to send one. That it is a very great reproach to America, to say there is only one General in it. ... That the Head can't possibly be sound when the whole body is disordered." The author concluded his remarks with religious fervor: "That the people of America have been guilty of Idolatry by making a man their god—and that the God of Heaven and Earth will convince them by woeful experience that he is only a man. That no good may be expected from the standing Army until Baal & his worshipers are banished from the Camp."

While these accusations were making their way through the Continental Congress, Conway had been transferred to Washington's staff at Valley Forge. Needless to say, this made for quite a bit of tension, and Washington confided to the Marquis de Lafayette on December 31, 1777, "[General Gates] became my inveterate Enemy; and has, I am persuaded, practiced every Art to do me an injury, even at the expense of reprobating a measure, which did not succeed, that he himself advised to. How far he may have accomplished his ends, I know not, and, but for considerations of a public Nature, I care not. For it is well known, that neither ambitious, nor lucrative motives led me to accept my present Appointments; in the discharge of which, I have endeavoured to observe one steady and uniform conduct, which I shall invariably pursue, while I have the honour to command, regardless of the Tongue of slander or the powers of detraction. The fatal tendency of disunion is so obvious, that I have, in earnest terms, exhorted such Officers as have expressed their dissatisfaction at General Conway's promotion, to be cool and dispassionate in their decision upon the matter; and I have hopes that they will not suffer any hasty determination to injure the service. At the same time, it must be acknowledged that Officers' feelings upon these occasions are not to be restrained, although you may control their

Actions."

Lafayette

This letter, and others like it, led Lafayette to take matters into his own hands and intervene on Washington's behalf. In January 1778, he traveled to the Continental Congress to speak in his dear friend's defense, telling the legislators that France considered Washington to be synonymous with the American cause. Lafayette's remarks strongly implied that, should the General be removed, there would be little hope of France assisting the colonies in their fight against Great Britain. This was enough to silence all critics, as the fledgling country was desperate for French help (which would not come until the formal alliance was reached in February 1778). While Conway and Gates would continue to work behind the scenes to remove Washington, no one in authority publicly spoke ill of Washington again.

Though his detractors may have been silenced, Washington still had to fight his own demons of self-doubt, which led to one of the most enduring but possibly apocryphal moments of that winter. According to Reverend Nathaniel Snowden, Isaac Potts, whose house Washington lived in while at Valley Forge, told the reverend decades later that he had seen Washington kneeling and praying in the snow in the woods. Snowden wrote in a journal what Potts allegedly told him: "I tied my horse to a sapling & went quietly into the woods & to my astonishment I saw the great George Washington on his knees alone, with his sword on one side and his cocked hat on the other. He was at Prayer to the God of the Armies, beseeching to interpose with his Divine aid, as it was ye Crisis, & the cause of the country, of humanity & of the world. Such a prayer I never heard from the lips of man. I left him alone praying. I went home & told my wife. I saw a sight and heard today what I never saw or heard before, and just related to her what I had seen & heard & observed. We never thought a man c'd be a soldier & a Christian, but if there is one in the world, it is Washington. She also was astonished. We thought it was the cause of God, & America could prevail."

The legend has since spread, and artist John McRae's painting of Washington praying in the snow remains popular, but the story is likely not authentic. For one thing, Snowden's family didn't move to Valley Forge until the 19th century, and there's no indication he knew Potts at all. Moreover, Washington typically stood up when he prayed, and as historian Gordon Wood noted, such an act was not in keeping with Washington's nature: "To be sure, he was conventionally liberal on matters of religion ('being no bigot myself to any mode of worship'), and though he went to church regularly to keep up decorum, he was not an emotionally religious person. He rarely mentioned Christ in his writings, and he usually referred to God as 'the great disposer of human events.'"

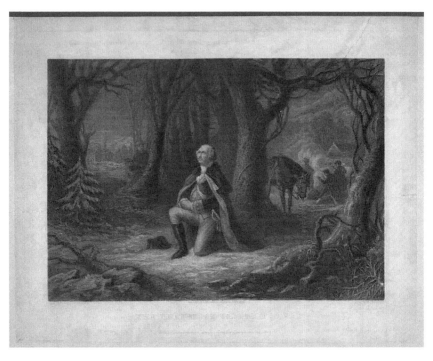

McRae's painting of Washington kneeling at Valley Forge

What is known is that Washington did indeed use Isaac Potts' house as his headquarters, and it remains one of the most toured spots in Valley Forge National Historical Park.

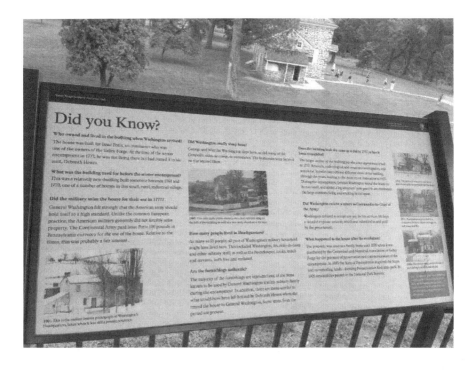

Did you Know?

Who owned and lived in the building when Washington arrived?

The house was built for Isaac Potts, an ironmaster who was one of the owners of the Valley Forge. At the time of the winter encampment in 1777, he was not living there but had rented it to his aunt, Deborah Hewes.

What was the building used for before the winter encampment?

This was a relatively new dwelling built sometime between 1768 and 1770, one of a number of houses in this small, rural, industrial village.

Did the military seize the house for their use in 1777?

General Washington felt strongly that the American army should hold itself to a high standard. Unlike the common European practice, the American military generally did not forcibly seize property. The Continental Army paid Isaac Potts 100 pounds in Pennsylvania currency for the use of the house. Relative to the times, this was probably a fair amount.

Did Washington really sleep here?

George and Martha Washington slept here, as did many of the General's aides-de-camp, or assistants. The bedrooms were located on the second floor.

How many people lived in Headquarters?

As many as 25 people, all part of Washington's military household, might have lived here. This included Washington, his aides-de-camp and other military staff, as well as the Housekeeper, cooks, maids and servants, both free and enslaved.

Are the furnishings authentic?

The majority of the furnishings are reproductions of the items known to be used by General Washington and his military family during the encampment. In addition, there are items similar to what would have been left behind by Deborah Hewes when she turned the house to General Washington. Some items from the period are genuine.

Does the building look the same as it did in 1777, or has it been remodeled?

The larger portion of the building (to the right) appears much as it did. However, a physiological and structural investigation, and analysis of building materials, offers different views of the building, through the years leading to the most recent restoration in 1905. During the encampment, General Washington found the house to be too small, and added a log structure (now gone) to accommodate the large numbers living and working in this space.

Did Washington receive a salary as Commander-in-Chief of the Army?

Washington refused to accept any pay for his services. He kept a detailed expense account, which was submitted to and paid by the government.

What happened to the house after the revolution?

The property was used as a family home until 1878 when it was purchased by the Centennial and Memorial Association of Valley Forge for the purpose of preservation and commemoration of the encampment. In 1893 the State of Pennsylvania acquired the house and surrounding lands - forming Pennsylvania's first state park. In 1976 ownership passed to the National Park System.

1865. This is the earliest known photograph of Washington's Headquarters, taken when it was still a private residence.

Pictures of Washington's headquarters

A barn and stables on the Potts' property

Picture of the office room for aides-de-camp in Washington's headquarters

Pictures of the office room believed to have been used by Washington in his headquarters

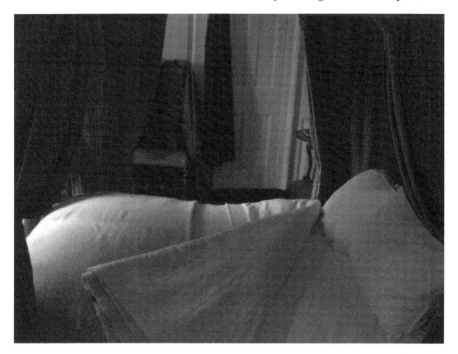

Pictures of the room believed to have been Washington's bedroom at his headquarters

Pictures of the bedroom believed to be used by Washington's aides

Picture of the attic

Pictures of the kitchen

Picture of a trap door above the kitchen believed to have been used to house slaves

A statue of Washington depicted as Cincinnatus near the headquarters

Replicas of the log huts used by Washington's guard near the headquarters

Chapter 5: Relieve the Gloom

"But the picture, though a dark one, had its lights as well as shadows. The men had their seasons of out-door sport and recreation, and not infrequently some private hut was the scene of uproarious merriment and boisterous hilarity. Innocent games were encouraged for amusement, and while cards and dice were forbidden, as leading to gambling, other means were found or invented with which to while away in pleasure the hours in which the men were not on duty, or taking their needed rest. The officers also had their fetes and entertainments, the few ladies of the camp, conspicuously the wives of Generals Knox and Greene, contributing their share to the brilliancy and success of such occasions. Washington and his wife were sometimes present at these as guests of honor. By visiting the huts, also, and ministering in various ways to the needs of the sick and unfortunate men, these good ladies, with Martha Washington in the lead, while in camp, did much to relieve the gloom and hardship of the dreary winter." - James Riddle, *Valley Forge Guide and Handbook* (1910)

Though conditions in camp had improved somewhat by February 1778, getting supplies to feed and clothe his men remained a thorn in Washington's side throughout the winter. On February 7, he wrote, "The occasional deficiencies in the Article of Provisions, which we have often severely felt, seem now on the point of resolving themselves into this fatal Crisis, total want and a dissolution of the Army. Mr. Blaine informs me, in the most decisive terms, that he has not the least prospect of answering the demands of the Army, within his district, more than a month longer, at the extremity. The expectations, he has from other Quarters, appear to be altogether vague and precarious; and from anything I can see, we have every reason to apprehend the most ruinous consequences. The spirit of desertion among the Soldiery, never before rose to such a threatening height, as at the present time. The murmurs on account of Provisions are become universal, and what may ensue, if a better prospect does not speedily open, I dread to conjecture. I pretend not to assign the causes of the distress, we experience in this particular, nor do I wish to throw out the least imputation of blame upon any person. I only mean to represent our affairs as they are, that necessity may be properly felt, of exerting the utmost care and activity, to prevent the mischiefs, which I cannot forbear anticipating, with inexpressible concern."

Even worse, the British knew how bad things were and sensed that they might be able to win the war simply by waiting the Americans out. On February 12, General James Varnum conceded "that in all human probability the army must dissolve. Many of the troops are destitute of meat and are several days in arrears. The horses are dying for want of forage. The country in the vicinity of the camp is exhausted. There cannot be a moral certainty of bettering our condition while we remain here, what consequences have we rationally to expect?" That same week, Washington admitted in a letter to Governor George Clinton, "For some days past there has been little less than a famine in camp. A part of the army has been a week without any kind of flesh, and the rest three or four days. Naked and starved as they are, we cannot enough admire the incomparable patience and fidelity of the soldiery, that they have not been, ere this, excited by their sufferings to general mutiny and desertion."

However, something changed at Valley Forge on February 10, which the British either knew nothing of or did not appreciate. On that day, Washington's much beloved wife, Martha, arrived from Virginia. The two had not seen each other since the war began over 2 years earlier, and George had missed his "Patsy" sorely. She brought with her a bustling, optimistic sense of home, telling him tales of his dear Mount Vernon and their growing family. She also brought with her a sense of organization and management that came from decades of helping George run a large plantation. She soon began to organize the other women who had traveled to be with their husbands into useful committees to knit socks and patch and mend worn out uniforms.

While Martha brought some supplies with her, there was still not nearly enough for everyone. Washington wrote to Patrick Henry on February 19, "The melancholy prospect before us, with respect to supplies of provisions, induces me, reluctantly to trouble you on a subject, which does not naturally fall within the circle of your attention. The situation of the Commissary's department and of the army, in consequence, is more deplorable, than you can easily imagine.

We have frequently suffered temporary want and great inconveniences, and for several days past, we have experienced little less than a famine in camp; and have had much cause to dread a general mutiny and dispersion. Our future prospects are, if possible, still worse: The magazines laid up, as far as my information reaches, are insignificant, totally incompetent to our necessities, and from every appearance, there has been heretofore so astonishing a deficiency in providing, that unless the most vigorous and effectual measures are at once, everywhere adopted, the language is not too strong to declare, that we shall not be able to make another campaign."

When one reads this letter, it's clear that Washington seemed to have more vigor and determination, possibly due to the comfort of having his wife near. Whereas he had been more disconsolate in his previous letters, now he demanded to know the reason for the deficiencies: "To what causes this is to be attributed; whether to an ill-timed and too general revolution in the department, in the midst of a campaign, to its being placed in improper hands, or to a diminution of resources and increased difficulties in the means of procuring, or to a combination of all these circumstances, I shall not undertake to decide. We have to lament that our affairs are so situated, and it is incumbent upon us, to employ our utmost efforts to ward off the ruin such a situation of things threatens. We have it in our power to do it; but our greatest activity and the fullest exertion of our resources, are requisite. I am earnestly requesting the aid of the executive authority of those States, whence our supplies are drawn; and in pursuance of this intention, I address myself to you; convinced that our alarming distresses will engage your most serious consideration; and that the full force of that zeal and vigour you have manifested upon every other occasion, will now operate for our relief, in a matter that so nearly affects the very existence of our contest. What methods you have it in your power to embrace for this purpose, your own judgment will best suggest; the substance of my present request, is, that you will contribute your assistance to turning all the supplies your State can afford, more than are sufficient for the subsistence of its inhabitants, into a channel of supplies for the army, in such a way as will appear to you most effectual; and at the same time to forwarding the means of transportation, from a defect in which we suffer great embarrassments."

For her part, Martha remained positive and optimistic, writing to a friend shortly after her arrival, "I came to this place about the first of February where I found the General very well—I left my Children at our House…. The General is camped in what is called the great Valley on the Banks of the Schuykill officers and men are chiefly in Hutts, which they say is tolerable comfortable; the army are as healthy as can well be expected in general—the Generals apartment is very small he has had a log cabin built to dine in which has made our quarter much more tolerable than they were at first"

With Martha's encouragement, George offered the wives, mothers and sisters who lived in the camp half-rations, to be provided by the Continental Congress, in return for their work doing laundry and sewing. He also encouraged the men to spend some of their free time with the children that also came to the camp with their mothers, and he even authorized the little ones to receive quarter rations from the already slim supplies. In doing this, Washington recognized that families provided much needed emotional support.

During the winter, as many as 500 women lived in the camp at some point in time. While most were wives and other family members, a few were prostitutes, a situation to which the Washington's chose to turn a blind eye. Another task to which the women turned their hands that winter was nursing the sick. This was critical, as one of the camp's doctors, James Thatcher, confided in his journal: "[I]t was with the greatest difficulty that men enough could be found in a fit condition to discharge the military camp duties from day to day, and for this purpose, those who were naked borrowed of those more fortunate of their comrades who had clothes. The army, indeed, was not without consolation, for his Excellency, the Commander-in-Chief, whom every soldier venerates and loves, manifested a parental concern and fellow-feeling for their sufferings, and made every exertion in his power to remedy the evil and to administer the much desired relief."

Under Martha's leadership, the women in the camp organized small parties and concerts during the winter and even once persuaded some of the soldiers to put on a play. Decades later, one of the women, a Mrs. Westlake, recalled, "I never in my life knew a woman so busy from early morning until late at night as was Lady Washington, providing comforts for the sick soldiers. Every day, excepting Sundays, the wives of officers in camp, and sometimes other women, were invited to Mr. Potts to assist her in knitting socks, patching garments, and making shirts for the poor soldiers when materials could be procured. Every fair day she might be seen, with basket in hand, and with a single attendant, going among the huts seeking the keenest and most needy sufferers, and giving all the comfort to them in her power. I sometimes went with her, for I was a stout girl, sixteen years old. On one occasion she went to the hut of a dying sergeant, whose young wife was with him. His case seemed to particularly touch the heart of the good lady, and after she had given him some wholesome food she had prepared with her own hands, she knelt down by his straw pallet and prayed earnestly for him and his wife with her sweet and solemn voice. I shall never forget the scene."

Chapter 6: The Birthplace of the United States Army

"The camp also now and then had its gala days, or days of great general rejoicing. Such was the 5th of May, when the news reached camp that France had acknowledged the independence of the young republic, and had formed with her a treaty of commerce and friendly alliance. As the news spread through the encampment loud and prolonged shouts and cheers shook the forests that shrouded the hills; and the day following, a day set apart for special thanksgiving to Almighty God in honor of the event, salutes were fired, and by direction of the Commander-in-Chief the whole army shouted: 'Huzzah for the King of France!' The coming of spring with its genial weather had the effect also of infusing new heart and hope into both men and officers, and in spite of the sickness and death that prevailed in the weeks that followed life in camp took on a more cheery aspect. Men who for lack of blankets and clothing had been obliged at times to sit up all night by the fire, to keep from freezing, might now be seen knocking the clay or mortar from the chinks between the logs of their huts to let in the warm air; while picket service and the usual round of out-door duty, no longer a dreaded task, became a welcome exercise." - James Riddle, *Valley Forge Guide and Handbook* (1910)

One of the issues the presence of women could not solve was the lack of pay for the soldiers. Not only were the soldiers not being fed and clothed, they were not even being paid the money Congress had promised them when they enlisted. As a result, many had deserted, or more precisely had taken advantage of authorized furloughs to get away and not return. Washington hoped that Patrick Henry could help him lure his forces back: "I am duly honoured with your favour of the 28th of last month. The method of paying the additional state bounty that appears to me most eligible is that of sending the money to Camp, with a temporary paymaster, to be issued on Warrants from me, agreeable to muster rolls and abstracts, authenticated in the same manner as practiced in other cases. Any other mode, however, that may be deemed more convenient, will be perfectly agreeable to me. I submit it to consideration, whether it might not be advisable for your Excellency, to issue a notification to those Soldiers, who have been reenlisted and permitted to go home on furlough, that on their return to Camp, they will receive the additional bounty, as prescribed by the Act of Assembly. As most of them engaged before the Act took place or was announced, the bounty may be put upon the footing of a reward for past services. This notification may have an influence in making them more faithful and punctual in returning to Camp at the expiration of their furloughs."

As the winter wore on, Washington took time in camp to regroup and think about the future. He was very fortunate at this point to have Baron Friedrich von Steuben in charge of training his troops. Though the men were often cold and hungry, the Prussian drillmaster pushed them outside each day to practice the skills that could save their lives and win battles. Under von Steuben's direction, the men were transformed that winter from raw recruits into polished soldiers.

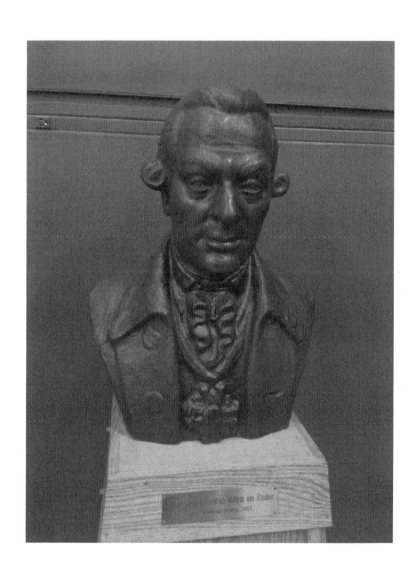

Pictures of a bust and statue of von Steuben at Valley Forge

Pictures of the parade ground used to drill soldiers at Valley Forge

An illustration depicting von Steuben drilling soldiers

During this time, Washington also began recruiting Native Americans to fight on behalf of the colonies. This was tricky business, as he had himself fought against two decades earlier as a British soldier during the French and Indian War. However, he was open to the possibility that former enemies could become allies, writing on March 13, 1778, "You will perceive, by the enclosed Copy of a Resolve of Congress, that I am empowered to employ a body of four hundred Indians, if they can be procured upon proper terms. Divesting them of the Savage customs exercised in their Wars against each other, I think they may be made of excellent use, as scouts and light troops, mixed with our own Parties…I propose to raise about one half the number among the Southern and the remainder among the Northern Indians. I have sent Colonel Nathanial Gist, who is well acquainted with the Cherokees and their Allies, to bring as many as he can from thence, and I must depend upon you to employ suitable persons to procure the stipulated number or as near as may be from the Northern tribes. The terms made with them should be such as you think we can comply with, and persons well acquainted with their language, manners and Customs and who have gained an influence over them should accompany them. The Oneidas have manifested the strongest attachment to us throughout this dispute and I therefore suppose, if any can be procured, they will be most numerous. Their Missionary Mr. Kirkland seemed to have an uncommon ascendency over that tribe and I should therefore be glad to see him accompany them. If the Indians can be procured, I would choose to have them here by the opening of the Campaign, and therefore they should be engaged as soon as possible as there is not more time between this and the Middle of May than will be necessary to settle the business with them and to March from their Country to the Army. I am not without hopes that this will reach you before the treaty which is to be held, breaks up. If it should, you will have an Opportunity of knowing their sentiments, of which I shall be glad to be informed, as soon as possible."

As it turned out, Washington was never able to recruit a significant number of Native Americans to his army. He wrote on May 3, "In a late letter from General Schuyler, I received the proceedings of a Board of Commissioners for Indian affairs…It appears by them, and some other accounts, I have seen, that there is very little prospect of succeeding in the plan, for engaging a body of Indians from that quarter to serve with this army."

The problem, it turned out, was not one of loyalty but of money, as Washington noted: "The advantage, which the enemy possess over us, in having the means of making presents, much more liberally than we can, has made a strong impression upon their Minds, and seems to be more than a counter balance, for any arguments we can offer to conciliate their attachments."

Then there was the matter of the atrocities some villages had suffered at the hands of the Americans. This led Washington to observe, "They also appear to be apprehensive for their own safety, and rather to wish for aid and protection from us, than willing to leave their habitations and come to our assistance."

Ultimately, he concluded, "The measure proposed was by way of experiment, as one, which might possibly be attended with valuable consequences; and if it could have been effected, without much difficulty, might have been worth a trial. But as the scheme does not well correspond with their present disposition and may serve to increase our embarrassments, in keeping them even in tolerable good humour, I am inclined to think it would be most advisable to relinquish the attempt. They may be told of what has happened in Europe, with proper embellishments, and that our affairs are now upon such a footing as to render their aid, in the field unnecessary, and that all we require of them is their friendship and good wishes. This and promises of protection may have a very powerful and happy effect. It is of great importance to counteract the temptations held out by the enemy, and to secure the good will of the Indians, who appear at least to be in a state of hesitancy and indecision, if nothing worse. Congress, I am persuaded will do every thing in their power to promote these desireable ends."

Though things did not work out with the Native Americans, Washington received another boost as the dreadful winter came to an end. With spring arrived the news that France had indeed agreed to join the fight for American freedom and would be sending men and supplies as soon as it could be arranged. This information sent waves of hope throughout the beleaguered camp and a formal celebration was held on May 6. After marching in formation and showing off to the General the skills they had mastered over the winter, the men each retired to their huts to enjoy an extra ration of rum.

As Washington prepared in May to break camp and continue fighting, he was able to leave in an orderly, newly revived manner. He gave the following orders: "A Surgeon from each brigade is to remain in camp to attend the sick which shall be left behind, under the direction of Dr. Hutchinson, till relieved by surgeons from the General Hospital, when they are to immediately join their respective regiments. Men with the small-pox, or under inoculation, are to be comprehended in the number of the sick. Commanding officers of regiments will assist the regimental surgeons in procuring as many women of the army as can be prevailed on to serve as nurses to them, for which they will be paid the usual price. Orderlies are also to be left, one to every 20 sick men, who are to be such as, for want of clothing…and the like, are least fit to march with the army, but at the same time capable of this duty. A commissary is likewise to be left to supply the sick with provisions. A commissioned officer to every 50 men is to remain, and a field-officer to superintend the whole. The arms of the sick in each regiment are to supply, as &r as necessary, the deficiency of those unfit for duty. If any remain, they are to be left in care of the officer who stays with the sick."

Moreover, by this time, Washington could feel confident that those he left behind would have enough to eat, as that spring saw an unusually large movement of shad up the Schuylkill River.

The winter at Valley Forge remains legendary in military history both for its severity and its results. In the end, the time that the American troops spent there proved to be critical to the future of the American colonies. While many died and others deserted, those that remained were closer to each other than they had ever been before, becoming true brothers in arms in a way that only privation and desperation could produce. Perhaps more importantly, von Steuben succeeded in transforming forces consisting mostly of inexperienced militia patched together into a professional army that could fight the British on open ground. The Prussian veteran would later note that the "enterprise succeeded better than…expected," and today the Valley Forge National Historical Park bills the site as "the birthplace of the United States Army."

Most arrived in the camp in December 1777 as Pennsylvanians or Virginians or New Yorkers, but they left in June 1778 as Americans, dedicated to a common cause that would unite them not just for the rest of the war but for the decades that followed. This dedication would see them through battles with bullets and with words, as each man, woman and child contributed their own part to creating the American dream. Before leaving their winter encampment, the officers who had survived took an oath that would shape all their future dealings, both as part of the army and of the new nation. Each man stated, in the presence of his peers, "I do acknowledge the UNITED STATES of AMERICA to be Free, Independent and Sovereign States, and declare that the people thereof owe no allegiance or obedience to George the Third, King of Great Britain ; and I renounce, refuse and abjure any allegiance or obedience to him; and I do Swear that I will, to the utmost of my power, support, maintain and defend the said United States against the said King George the Third, his heirs and successors, and his or their abettors, assistants and adherents, and will serve the said United States in the office of Lieutenant which I now hold, with fidelity, according to the best of my skill and understanding."

Pictures of Valley Forge National Historical Park

Equestrian statue of General Anthony Wayne

Pictures of General Knox's headquarters

The National Memorial Arch

Pictures of the Washington Memorial Chapel

A monument to the soldiers erected by the Daughters of the American Revolution

Statues commemorating the Army's officers

The Masons' monument at Valley Forge

The New Jersey monument

The Massachusetts monument

Pictures of an original redoubt and trench along the inner line of the Valley Forge encampment

Picture of the artillery position along the inner line

Picture of Artillery Park, where artillery was kept at the camp

Online Resources

Other Revolutionary War titles by Charles River Editors

Other books about Valley Forge on Amazon

Bibliography

Fleming, Thomas. (2005). Washington's Secret War: The Hidden History of Valley Forge. Washington, D.C. Smithsonian.

Freedman, Russell (2008). Washington at Valley Forge. New York: Holiday House.

Riddle, James. (1910). Valley Forge Guide and Handbook. Philadelphia: J. B. Lippincott Company.

Trussell Jr., John B. B. (1976). Birthplace of an Army: A Study of the Valley Forge Encampment. Harrisburg, PA: Pennsylvania Historical and Museum Commission.